Librarian

Deborah Underwood

KIDHAVEN PRESS

An imprint of Thomson Gale, a part of The Thomson Corporation

THOMSON
™
GALE

Detroit • New York • San Francisco • San Diego
New Haven, Conn. • Waterville, Maine • London • Munich

© 2005 Thomson Gale, a part of The Thomson Corporation.

Thomson and Star Logo are trademarks and Gale and KidHaven Press are registered trademarks used herein under license.

For more information, contact
KidHaven Press
27500 Drake Rd.
Farmington Hills, MI 48331-3535
Or you can visit our Internet site at http://www.gale.com

LIBRARY OF CONGRESS CATALOGING-IN-PUBLICATION DATA

Underwood, Deborah.
    Librarian / by Deborah Underwood.
        p. cm.—(Exploring careers)
    Includes bibliographical references and index.
    ISBN 0-7377-2610-5
    1. Librarians—Juvenile literature. 2. Library science—Vocational guidance—Juvenile literature. 3. Libraries—Juvenile literature. I. Title. II. Exploring careers (KidHaven Press)
    Z682.U5125 2005
    020'.92—dc22

                                                                2004003742

Printed in the United States of America

CONTENTS

CHAPTER 1

Different Kinds of Librarians

In the children's room of a city library, a woman gathers toddlers and their parents together for story time. At a law school, a man teaches students how to find information they need for their classes. In an office downtown, a man working for a large corporation searches the Internet for news about a rival company. In a special museum vault, a woman carefully mends a rare book printed three hundred years ago. What do these people have in common? They are all librarians.

People often think librarians spend their days surrounded by books in school or public libraries. Many librarians do work in public libraries and schools. However, librarians can also be found working at radio stations, hospitals, museums, law firms, film studios, and government offices. Some librarians work with books, but others organize film clips, photographs, maps, or sheet music. Some work only with information stored on computers.

No matter where they work and what materials they handle, librarians help people find and use information. In the United States, about 150,000 books are published each year. There are thousands of different magazines, journals, and newspapers, and new issues of each appear regularly. New Web sites spring up every day. Librarians have the knowledge and skills to help people sort through this flood of information and find what they need.

A librarian helps university students find useful information for a research project.

Public Librarians

Public libraries can be found in big cities, small towns, and rural areas. A public librarian might work at a bustling reference desk, teach classes in researching on the Internet, or drive a bookmobile that brings library materials to people living in the country. Since public libraries are open to everyone, public librarians help people of all ages, races, and backgrounds. Some choose to work mainly with children, and some work with teens or adults.

Public librarians help patrons find answers to questions. What does a vampire bat eat? How do you say "house" in Italian? Who wrote *Pride and Prejudice*? How many jelly beans would fit in a bas-

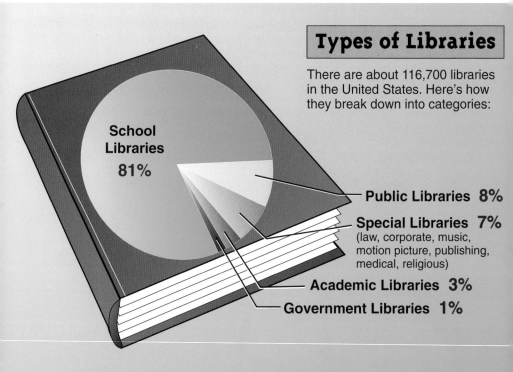

Types of Libraries

There are about 116,700 libraries in the United States. Here's how they break down into categories:

School Libraries
81%

Public Libraries 8%

Special Libraries 7%
(law, corporate, music, motion picture, publishing, medical, religious)

Academic Libraries 3%

Government Libraries 1%

SOURCE: American Library Association, 2004.

ketball? Librarians answer questions like these every day. In 1998, public librarians answered over 292,000,000 reference questions. People do not even need to leave home to get help from public librarians. During library hours, librarians answer questions by e-mail or telephone. In some places, people can log on to the Internet and get help from a librarian any time—even in the middle of the night!

Public librarians provide important services to their communities. They plan library programs that educate and entertain the public. Almost all libraries provide computer access, and librarians teach people how to use computers and the Internet. Public librarians organize many types of reading activities. These activities include book discussion groups for adults and summer reading programs for children. Librarians also plan special events such as puppet shows, concerts, and readings by authors.

School Librarians

School librarians, also called school library media specialists, work in public schools, private schools, and **parochial** (religious) **schools.** Whether a school librarian works in an elementary school or a high school, an important part of his or her job is teaching. Gail Bradley, an elementary school librarian, leads four or five classes a day. She teaches students how to use dictionaries, atlases, encyclopedias, phone books, and other reference sources.

An academic librarian teaches a group of college students how to use the library's resources to do research.

In addition, she introduces them to different types of books, from mysteries to folktales. She also shows students how to find books on the library shelves.

Some school librarians do not teach classes, but they still spend much of their time showing students how to do research. High school librarian Tom Jalbert helps students with class assignments and research papers. He also tries to make information easy for them to find. If he knows students are studying a certain subject, he will place books on that topic on a special cart. He sometimes prints out lists of books for students so they will know what to look for if they visit the public library.

Like other librarians, school librarians have a wide variety of tasks. When Bradley is not teaching classes, she might be checking the library shelves for outdated or damaged books, sending out overdue notices, organizing author visits, or supervising the fifty students who come to use the library during recess.

Academic Librarians

Academic librarians work in college or university libraries. Teaching students how to find information is often part of an academic librarian's job. Karen Beck, a librarian at a law school, spends nearly half her time on the job teaching law students how to do legal research. She shows her students how to use computers to find law cases and teaches them how to do research for the articles they write. She also helps professors find information needed to teach their classes and answers questions at the reference desk.

Many academic libraries contain collections of rare books or other historical items. Along with her other responsibilities, Beck is the **curator,** the person in charge, of the law school's rare book collection. She talks with rare book dealers and helps decide which books to buy. Putting together public exhibits of the rare books is one of her favorite jobs. As she explains, "I love to be among the books and think of all the lawyers from hundreds of years past who have handled these books and

A librarian wears protective gloves as he handles a rare book published in 1665.

used them in their lives. And the books themselves are very beautiful and very special. It's fun to be able to bring them into people's lives."[1]

Special Librarians

A special library is a library that focuses on a particular subject. There are over nine thousand special libraries in the United States. They can be found in a wide range of places, from art museums to zoos. Some companies and law firms have their own libraries. Special librarians are hired to run these libraries. For example, librarians who work for newspapers show reporters how to find facts needed for their stories. Government librarians help elected officials and members of the public find information.

Special libraries often contain books as well as **periodicals,** publications printed at fixed intervals, but some have other special collections related to their fields. The library at the Academy of Motion Picture Arts and Sciences in Beverly Hills, California, has a collection of sixty thousand film scripts and twenty-five thousand movie posters. It

A librarian in the motion picture division of the Library of Congress examines several reels of film.

also houses unique film-related items such as the wig the Cowardly Lion wore in the movie *The Wizard of Oz.*

Because special libraries focus only on certain subjects, they can cover those subjects in much greater depth than a general library could. Lawrence Currie, a librarian at a science museum, works with a large collection of books, maps, and journals that all relate to natural history. He points out that not many general libraries could buy an expensive book on single-celled plants because not many people would use it. However, in a special library focused on natural history, there would be greater demand for such a specific book.

Combining Interests

Librarians often choose to work in special libraries so they can combine their interest in books with interests in other subjects. A librarian who enjoys music might decide to work in a music library. A librarian interested in medicine might work at a hospital or medical center library.

No matter where librarians work, people turn to them for help when they need answers. Without librarians, the search for information would be slow, frustrating, and sometimes even impossible.

CHAPTER 2

What Do Librarians Do?

L ibrarians perform a wide range of tasks, both in public view and behind the scenes. A librarian in a large library might work in only one department. For example, he or she might focus on organizing magazines or answering reference questions. In a smaller library, a librarian might do everything from repairing books to planning special events. In the past, librarians worked mostly with books, magazines, and other printed material. Now they purchase and organize everything from compact discs to collections of computerized information called **databases.**

Helping People Find Information

A big part of most librarians' job is helping people find answers to questions. People visiting the library

A school librarian checks his computer to help answer a student's question.

go to the reference desk to ask questions. Others who need help telephone the library or send e-mail to librarians. Some librarians specialize in reference work and spend most of their time answering questions. Others work at the reference desk for only part of their day.

School librarians help students research homework questions. Medical librarians help doctors find information they need to care for their patients. Sometimes a librarian can help simply by pointing a patron toward the correct area of the library. However, sometimes a librarian must spend a lot of time looking for the right answer. Most librarians find the search for answers exciting. They compare it to going on a scavenger hunt or solving a challenging puzzle.

Librarians at the Lucasfilm Research Library provide information to people involved in movie and television production. If a movie is set in Chicago in the 1890s, the librarians might write detailed reports about that time period. This helps the screenwriter make the movie true to history. If a costume designer wants pictures of wedding dresses from 1954 or an artist wants photographs of African elephants, the librarians search through books, magazines, computer databases, and special file folders full of pictures to find what is needed.

Now that so much information is available online, sometimes library patrons find too much information. If someone searches the Internet for "whales," links to thousands of Web sites appear. Librarians can help people screen out information they do not need. High school librarian Tom Jalbert remembers

A reference librarian at a university helps a student search the Internet for Web sites.

a student who needed to know about a certain mythological character for a report he was writing. The student searched the Internet and came up with dozens of Web sites for companies named after the character—not much help for his report! Jalbert was able to help the student find a better way to get the facts he needed.

Teaching Groups and Individuals

Many academic and school librarians spend part of their time teaching classes. Elementary school librarian Lezlie Glare usually meets with six classes a day. She teaches her students everything from book appreciation to research skills. Some academic librarians teach ongoing classes about how to do research. Some hold sessions at the beginning of each school year to show college students how to use library resources.

Jalbert feels an important part of his job is teaching his students how to determine whether sources they find on the Internet are reliable: "Is the information from a university, or is it just from some student who put up his own Web site on biology?"[2] Since anyone can put up a Web site, Jalbert wants to make sure his students know whether the information they find online is accurate or not.

Public librarians and special librarians also sometimes teach. Because most library catalogs are computerized, a person who does not know how to use a computer will have trouble finding books. To help, many public libraries offer classes in basic computer skills. Even if formal classes are not offered, a public librarian might need to show a patron how to use the online catalog or even how to use a computer mouse. Special librarians sometimes teach staff members in their institutions how to use new databases and programs.

Sparking an Interest in Reading

Many school and children's librarians feel the most important part of their job is getting students excited about books and reading. Public librarians hold story hours for young children and host book-related

A children's librarian shares a book on sea life with an excited young boy.

Librarians set up this display in a Chicago bookstore to help encourage the public to read.

events. School librarians read to classes and teach students to appreciate books. Gail Bradley's favorite part of her job is sharing books with students: "If I'm excited about a book, I love to share it with them. I then try to follow up with those who have read what I suggested to see if they loved it as much as I did.

Another great part of the job is hearing the students tell me about a great book they have read."[3]

Librarians design special programs to encourage reading. Some public libraries offer summer reading programs that reward children for reading. Librarians from the San Francisco Public Library visit local schools to tell students about their program. Children keep track of which books they read and how many hours they spend reading. At the end of the summer, the children receive prizes such as free books or baseball caps for reading a certain number of hours.

Bradley and Glare help coordinate a Community Read at their school in Atherton, California. Everyone involved with the school—students, teachers, staff, and parents—reads the same book at the same time. The book is announced at a kickoff event each spring. Over the next weeks, students participate in a variety of activities related to the book. One year when the book was about a Mexican girl, events included a piñata party, a dance performance, and a fiesta with Mexican food and music.

Choosing What to Buy

Librarians are responsible for deciding which materials to buy for their libraries. They purchase not only books, but also videos, DVDs, compact discs, databases, and magazines. Librarians use lots of information to help them choose what to buy.

They read special journals filled with reviews of new books. They listen to requests from library users. They also notice which books library patrons use the most. If a librarian sees that children's picture books in Chinese are checked out often, he or she might make a note to order more.

School librarians talk with teachers to determine which materials students will need to do their research and reports. If eighth graders in a school study the Civil War, their librarian will try to make sure there are plenty of Civil War books in the library.

Special librarians also make sure to buy materials that meet the needs of their users. Since so much of the research that librarians at the Lucasfilm Research Library do is visual, librarian Jenny Craik says, "The main thing we're looking for when we purchase books is great photos."[4] If someone at Lucasfilm is working on a movie about a particular subject or period, Craik shops for books that will be useful to that person.

Working Behind the Scenes

Instead of working with the public, some librarians choose to work behind the scenes. Those who work in library management do things required to keep libraries running. They hire staff, manage finances, and plan for new library buildings.

Other librarians specialize in **cataloging**, a way of organizing materials. If the books in a library

How the Dewey Decimal System Works

Wild Animals of the World
590.3
Cole

Familiar Animals of America
591.54
Peck

Butterflies in the Backyard
Butterflies in the Backyard
595.78
Shaw

Main Category
Subcategories
Author's Name

Most public and school libraries in the United States catalog their books using the Dewey Decimal System. A book's catalog number (its call number) is like an address—it tells us where a book "lives" in the library, that is, which shelf it's on. The ten main categories in the Dewey system are:

000 Generalities
100 Philosophy and psychology
200 Religion
300 Social sciences
400 Language

500 Natural science and mathematics
600 Technology
700 Arts
800 Literature
900 Geography and history

were not organized, it could take hours to find anything. Fortunately, all libraries have systems in place to help patrons find what they need. But who decides where each book should be shelved? Should a book about the birds and fish of Florida be shelved with bird books, fish books, or Florida books? Catalogers study the books carefully and consult special reference materials to help them make these decisions.

Other behind-the-scenes librarians organize computerized information. A librarian might develop an online class that teaches people how to use Internet tools. Librarians design and maintain Web sites for their libraries, and sometimes even for their towns. They also make sure that online catalogs are simple to use.

Many Different Tasks

Some special librarians work to bring their libraries right into people's homes. They take digital photos of their collections and put the photos on Web sites so people all over the world can have access to them. Instead of having to travel across the country to see a rare book, a person might be able to look at it on a library's Web site.

With such a wide range of tasks to perform, most librarians find their jobs stimulating and enjoyable. Whether someone wants to teach children, preserve old books, answer questions, or assist scientists, there is a library job to fit his or her interests.

CHAPTER 3

What It Takes to Be a Librarian

Most librarians say their love of books and reading led them to pursue library work. Many fondly remember the time they spent in libraries as children. Library jobs offer a flexibility that appeals to many prospective librarians. Librarians can find jobs nearly everywhere, and there are many part-time library jobs.

After deciding to become a librarian, a person must get the required training. Some librarians begin working as library assistants and work their way up to librarian positions. But for most people, the journey to becoming a librarian begins with earning a college degree and then attending library school.

Training for a Career as a Librarian

No particular college degree is needed to enter library school. Librarians need a broad base of knowledge, so the more subjects a librarian knows, the better. Students interested in working in a special library may major in a related field in college. For example, someone wanting to work in an art library might get a college degree in art history. Someone who wants to work as a cataloger might major in a foreign language, since catalogers often process books and periodicals written in different languages.

Some librarians earn graduate degrees in other fields before they attend library school. A law librarian with both library and law degrees has more job opportunities, so many law librarians earn law degrees before entering library school. A music librarian might hold both a library degree and a graduate degree in music.

Because so much information is now in databases and on the Internet, students who hope to attend library school need good computer skills. They must be comfortable working online. Some library schools require their students to design Web sites. The student who knows Web design before entering one of these schools will have an advantage.

Pictured is a student studying in the library of the University of Redlands in California.

Library School

Most librarians who attend library school earn a Master of Library Science (MLS) degree. This degree sometimes goes by other names, such as Master of Library and Information Science (MLIS). A degree from one of the fifty-six schools **accredited**

Because many library resources are found on the computer, librarians must have strong computer skills.

(approved) by the American Library Association gives a librarian the best job opportunities.

Most MLS programs take from one to two years to complete. Some students choose to attend library school part-time. Since they may work during the day and take classes at night, these students may take three years or even longer to receive a degree.

Some library schools offer distance learning programs. In these programs, students can earn a library degree even if they do not live near a library school. They log on to online classes and talk to their teachers and fellow students over the Internet. Students in some programs spend a week on campus during the summer. In other programs, students spend three to five days on campus each term. Still others allow students to earn MLS degrees without ever leaving home.

Types of Courses

Most library schools have certain courses that all students must take. In the first year of library school, students learn about the history of books and the role of information in society. They study ways to organize information, how to select materials, and how to do reference work.

After taking the required courses, library students choose additional courses in their special areas of interest. These courses help them prepare for the particular type of library work they wish to

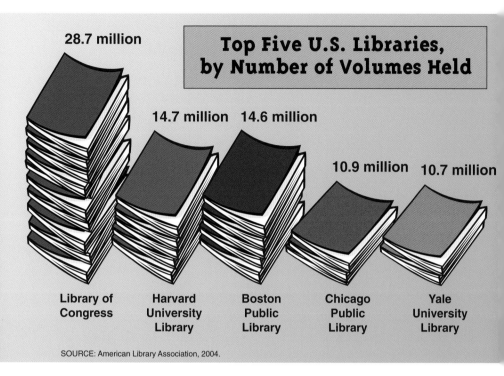

Top Five U.S. Libraries, by Number of Volumes Held

28.7 million

14.7 million   14.6 million

10.9 million   10.7 million

| Library of Congress | Harvard University Library | Boston Public Library | Chicago Public Library | Yale University Library |

SOURCE: American Library Association, 2004.

do. A student might take a course in cataloging or one in maintaining **archives**, which are collections of records or documents. Students can learn about how to manage library branches, how to work with government documents, or how to pick library books for teens.

Since school librarians often teach classes, someone training to be a school librarian must learn about teaching as well as library work. Some states require that school librarians also be licensed teachers in another subject.

Continuing to Learn

Even after they graduate from library school, librarians continue to learn. Professional organizations bring librarians together so they can learn from each other. There are separate groups for school librarians, children's librarians, special librarians, public librarians, reference librarians, law librarians, and nearly every other type of librarian. For example, the Young Adult Library Services Association works to strengthen library services to teenagers and to support librarians who work with teens.

Many of these groups hold yearly meetings or conferences. Librarians spend several days at these conferences learning more about their fields. A school librarian might attend a session about new ways to teach reading or one about new books for children. Public librarians might go to sessions about how to better help library users who do not speak English, or about how to raise money for their libraries. At these meetings, librarians from around the country share ideas with each other.

Ongoing Skill Development

Librarians sometimes attend one-day classes to help them learn new skills. If a library subscribes to a new database, librarians might go to a class to learn how to use it. Other classes might focus on how to work with library volunteers, how to prevent injuries on the job, or how to teach computer skills to library patrons.

Even if they do not attend classes or conferences, librarians keep learning. As they answer questions on the job, they add to their own knowledge. One thing that many librarians love about their career is the opportunity to learn new things every day. Every time a patron asks a new question, a librarian has a chance to learn.

Qualities a Librarian Needs

Because helping others and sharing information is a large part of library work, librarians must work well with people. People of all ages, cultural backgrounds, and educational levels use libraries. In the course of a day, a librarian might assist a child with homework research, help a tourist check e-mail, and work with other librarians to organize a library

A librarian and her staff spend part of their workday opening boxes of donated books.

event. Public librarians in particular need to be comfortable working with many kinds of people.

Most librarians perform a wide variety of duties, which means they must be flexible. They need to be able to switch between tasks quickly. For school librarian Lezlie Glare, "A typical day means meeting with six classes, preparing for the next day, and it may include ordering, cataloging, planning for visiting authors, working on grants, coordinating volunteers, attending meetings, and countless other things."[5] Librarians must put the needs of library patrons first, but still find time to do the things needed to keep their libraries running.

Librarians must be patient and organized to find the answers to difficult questions. Sometimes a librarian will spend hours seeking the answer to a single question. A librarian cannot give up when answers are hard to find. He or she must have a logical system for finding information.

For someone with the right interests, training, and qualities, a library career can be tremendously rewarding. Someone who likes reading books, using computers, and helping people might find that being a librarian is the perfect job.

CHAPTER 4

Meet a Librarian

Kathleen Keeler has fond memories of the bookmobile that came to her neighborhood when she was a child. Every week it parked down the street from her house, and Keeler visited it regularly. It felt like her own private library. She checked out books and participated in the library's summer reading programs. Now, as a children's librarian for the San Francisco Public Library, she helps run the summer reading program for her library branch. She also helps children select books, just as the bookmobile librarians helped her choose books when she was a girl.

Keeler has been a librarian for fourteen years, but being a librarian is a second career for her. She received a college degree in speech pathology and worked for five years helping people with speech difficulties. Her favorite part of that job was working with children. That fact, combined with her love of books, prompted her to return to school to get a library degree. As Keeler comments, "I'm amazed that I didn't think of a library career the

A children's librarian helps a group of children find books that interest them.

first time around, because it's the perfect job for me. The minute I thought of it, I knew it was what I wanted to do. I've always loved to read, and this is a good career for a reader."[6]

Two Important Responsibilities

A children's librarian does many different tasks every day. Of these, Keeler feels that answering children's questions and recommending books are her two most important responsibilities:

> Every day that I work, I answer reference questions. A lot of the questions that a children's librarian answers involve homework assignments. Children also ask questions about things they are interested in, like mummies, folding paper airplanes, spooky stories, and how to take care of pets. Today one child wanted to know about glow-worms. Another wanted to know what the letters J.K. in J.K. Rowling stand for. [The answer is Joanne Kathleen.] A third wanted to know what day of the week his birthday would be on in the year 2012!
>
> Another big part of the job is suggesting books to kids. When a child asks me to recommend a book, I ask them to tell me the name of some books they have read that they liked. Then I try to think of some other books similar to those. I also like to tell

children about some of my favorite books. I describe the book, especially the exciting parts, but I don't give away the ending so the child will want to read it to find out what happens.

No Typical Day

One of the things Keeler enjoys about her job is that the days are so varied. She does everything from attending committee meetings to holding story times for preschoolers. Like most public librarians, Keeler sometimes works evenings and weekends.

A children's librarian reads a storybook to a captivated group of young listeners.

Shelving books is just one of the many responsibilities of public librarians.

She is based in one branch of the library, but she works in other branches as well. Even though she is a children's librarian, she sometimes works in the adult section of the library.

Keeler does lots of work out of the public view. She and the other children's librarians put together reading lists to distribute to children. Every month she reads new children's books and reviews them to help the library system decide which books to purchase. Because Keeler is a children's book author herself, she brings special knowledge to her purchase suggestions. Sometimes before the library opens, she hosts class visits, giving students a tour of the library. She also looks through the books in the library's collection to see if they are out of date or in bad condition. If so, they will be removed from the shelves.

Finding time to do all these jobs is one of Keeler's challenges. As she explains, "There is a lot to do to keep the library running. Sometimes it is hard to find enough time to order books, plan programs, help patrons, decorate the library for holidays, visit nearby schools, supervise the children that volunteer at our branch, and serve on committees. It is a job that keeps you busy!"

A Creative Career

One of the things Keeler enjoys about her career is that librarians are able to bring their creative talents to the job. One of her coworkers does all the art projects and displays that decorate the children's room of the library. Another folds origami cranes to hang from the ceiling. Librarians with musical skills sing or play instruments during story times. When Keeler visits local schools to tell them about the library's summer reading program, she uses her own artistic gift: "I like to tell stories, so when I do the school visits, I learn a new story to tell the kids in the schools. That's always really fun—acting the story out, and seeing from the kids' expressions how interested they are."

Keeler also helps plan some of the many free public events her library branch offers:

A school librarian has the help of two volunteers to make story time fun for her young listeners.

Because I'm a children's librarian, I help plan special programs for kids. Sometimes the programs involve music, or dance, or puppets.

The programs are a nice service for kids and families. At this branch, we also offer several story times. Once a month we show films of children's books.

The best-attended program I ever gave was "Murder Mystery at the Library." Kids scoured the library looking for clues as to which suspect killed the victim. The clues were hidden in books to introduce the kids to the different types of books. We had to stop letting kids in after we reached 100 participants!

Many Rewards

Like any job, library work has challenges. Keeler remembers evenings when the power in the library went out and she had to lead people to the door with flashlights! Some difficulties are more predictable, such as budget problems and changing technology. As she explains:

> When the city and state have budget cuts, we don't have enough money to buy all the books that would be useful or subscribe to all the online databases we'd like to. They also result in hiring freezes, so we have fewer people working to put away the books and help people with reference questions. And it is a challenge to keep up with technology. The library offers training and also allows us to attend courses on new databases. We

librarians talk to each other about what new online and print sources we discover.

A Sense of Achievement

But for most librarians, including Keeler, the rewards of the job far outweigh the difficulties. As she further explains:

> I love helping children find books that they love. I think my favorite thing is when kids come back and say, "That was a really good book you told me about!" Sometimes they come in and say, "Well, I liked your book, and you might like the book I just read," then they tell you about that.
>
> I also love the opportunities to be creative that this job provides. Helping people with their questions is always very satisfying. Solving a tough reference question gives me a great sense of achievement. Sometimes illustrators come in looking for pictures of certain things they need to draw, or writers need specific information, so a librarian can be a part of new books being created. When I work at the adult desk, people ask us for books on writing résumés, or on how to study for a test to be a teacher. Librarians help these patrons improve their lives. There are so many rewards.

N O T E S

Chapter 1: Different Kinds of Librarians

1. Karen Beck, interview by author, November 19, 2003.

Chapter 2: What Do Librarians Do?

2. Tom Jalbert, interview by author, November 25, 2003.

3. Gail Bradley, e-mail to author, November 24, 2003.

4. Jenny Craik, interview by author, January 29, 2004.

Chapter 3: What It Takes to Be a Librarian

5. Lezlie Glare, e-mail to author, November 21, 2003.

Chapter 4: Meet a Librarian

6. All quotes in Chapter 4: Kathleen Keeler, interview by author November 12, 2003, and e-mail to author January 13, 2004.

GLOSSARY

accredited: Meets certain standards set by an outside organization.

archive: A collection of papers, photographs, or other items.

cataloging: Organizing books and other materials into logical groups so that people can find them easily.

curator: A person in charge of a museum or archive.

database: A collection of computerized information.

periodical: A publication, such as a magazine, published at regular intervals.

parochial school: A school run by a church or other religious institution.

FOR FURTHER EXPLORATION

Books

Liza Burby, *A Day in the Life of a Librarian.* New York: PowerKids, 2001. Follows a public librarian through a typical workday.

Laura Leone, *Choosing a Career in Information Science.* New York: Rosen, 2002. Includes a chapter on the history of libraries, as well as profiles of various library jobs such as cataloger and archivist.

Catherine de la Peña McCook and Margaret Myers, *Opportunities in Library and Information Science Careers.* Chicago: VGM Career Books, 2002. Comprehensive look at the various kinds of libraries and library work.

Internet Sources

Linda W. Braun, "New Roles: A Librarian by Any Name," *Library Journal,* February 1, 2002. http://libraryjournal.reviewsnews.com/index.as p?layout=articlePrint&articleID=CA191647& publication=libraryjournal.

U.S. Department of Labor, Bureau of Labor Statistics, "Jobs for Kids Who Like Reading." www.bls.gov/k12/html/edu_read.htm.

Linda K. Wallace, "Places an MLS Can Take You," *American Libraries*, March 2002.www.ala.org/Content/NavigationMenu/Our_Association/Offices/Human_Resource_Development_and_Recruitment/Careers_in_Libraries1/al_mls.pdf.

Web Sites

American Library Association (www.ala.org). This organization for librarians has information about libraries, library careers, and current library-related issues.

Become a Librarian (www.becomealibrarian.org). This Web site, compiled by the Central Jersey Regional Library Cooperative, includes information about library jobs and profiles of many different librarians.

Library of Congress (www.loc.gov). This Web site for the largest library in the world includes online galleries, profiles of famous Americans, and "Ask a Librarian," an online reference service.

INDEX

PICTURE CREDITS

Cover photo: © Art Today, Inc.

© AP/Wide World Photos, 10, 11, 26, 30

© Annie Griffiths Belt/CORBIS, 17

Getty Images, 18, 36, 38

© Mark E. Gibson/CORBIS, 33

© John Henley/CORBIS, 8

© Robert Holmes/CORBIS, 25

© James Marshall/CORBIS, 5

© Jose Palaez, Inc./CORBIS, 14

© O'Brien Productions/CORBIS, 35

© Chuck Savage/CORBIS, 15

Steve Zmina, 21

ABOUT THE AUTHOR

Deborah Underwood writes nonfiction, fiction, and poetry for children. She grew up in Walla Walla, Washington, and received a bachelor's degree in philosophy from Pomona College in Claremont, California. She now lives in San Francisco. When she is not writing, she enjoys reading and singing in a chamber choir. This is her second book for KidHaven Press.